The Call of the Wild

Jack London

Abridged and adapted by Phil LeFaivre

Illustrated by Carol Stutz

A PACEMAKER CLASSIC

Fearon/Janus/Quercus
Belmont, California

Simon & Schuster Education Group

Pacemaker Classics

The Adventures of Huckleberry Finn
The Adventures of Tom Sawyer
The Call of the Wild
A Christmas Carol
Crime and Punishment
David Copperfield
The Deerslayer
Dr. Jekyll and Mr. Hyde
Ethan Frome
Frankenstein
Great Expectations
Heart of Darkness
The Hunchback of Notre Dame
Jane Eyre
The Jungle Book
The Last of the Mohicans

The Mayor of Casterbridge
Moby Dick
The Moonstone
O Pioneers!
The Prince and the Pauper
The Red Badge of Courage
Robinson Crusoe
The Scarlet Letter
A Tale of Two Cities
The Three Musketeers
The Time Machine
Treasure Island
20,000 Leagues Under the Sea
Two Years Before the Mast
The War of the Worlds
Wuthering Heights

Library of Congress Catalog Card Number: 92–72585

ISBN 0–8224–9338–1

Printed in the United States of America

10 9 8 7 6 5
MA

Contents

1 The Lesson

Buck did not read the newspapers. If he had, he would have known that trouble was brewing for strong, long-haired dogs like him. Gold had been found in the Arctic, so thousands of men were rushing north to make their fortunes. These men needed dogs, but not just any dogs. They wanted strong, heavy dogs like Buck to carry their loads. They also wanted dogs with thick, furry coats like Buck's that could withstand the cold and frost of the north country.

Buck lived in a big, sunny house in Santa Clara Valley, California. Judge Miller's place, it was called. It stood far back from the road, hidden among the bushes and poplar trees that surrounded it. A gravel driveway wound through the trees and up to the front of the house. Behind the house stretched a spacious lawn that seemed to go on forever. Yet one could tell that it did not from the orchards and berry patches that grew along its border. And beyond these were the kennels, the great stables, the servants' cottages, and the other buildings that belonged to the Miller family.

All of this was Buck's territory. Here he was born, and here he had lived for the four years of his life. Of course, there were other dogs on the property, but they did not count. Some—like Toots, the pug, and Ysabel, the Mexican hairless—lived dull, spoiled lives inside the house. They were hardly ever seen putting their noses out of doors. Then others, like the fox terriers, spent their lives outside, but they were kept in kennels.

Buck, on the other hand, was neither a house dog nor a kennel dog. Buck ruled both worlds. And his was a grand life. He would swim with the judge's sons and take walks with the judge's daughters. At night he lay at the judge's feet as he and the judge shared the warmth of the fireplace together. He was king—that is, king over all things on Judge Miller's place, including people.

Buck's father, Elmo, was a huge Saint Bernard who had been Judge Miller's most faithful friend. Now Buck was following in his father's footsteps. At 140 pounds, he was not as large as his father. His mother, Shep, was a smaller Scotch shepherd. Still, Buck was a strong, heavy dog. His size and dignity gave him the right to walk like royalty around the place. Yet he never let himself become a spoiled house pet. Hunting and racing had kept the fat off and the muscles hard.

That was Buck in the fall of 1897, when gold was

pulling men northward. But Buck did not know about the gold rush. Nor did he know that Manuel, the gardener, spelled danger. Manuel loved to gamble. Yet his wages were too small for such a hobby. His downfall was that he was always sure he would win. One fateful time, he did not.

The judge and his family were gone the night of Manuel's crime. No one saw the gardener take Buck through the orchard and off into the darkness. (Buck thought he was going for a walk.) And only one man saw Buck and Manuel arrive at the railroad track. This man talked with the gardener for some time. Then money passed between the two.

"Wrap up the goods," the man said gruffly. So Manuel wrapped a thick rope around Buck's collar, which Buck allowed him to do. Buck trusted the men he knew.

"Twist the rope, and you'll choke 'em," said Manuel. But when the rope was handed to the stranger, Buck growled angrily.

Around the judge's place, such a growl was an order. But to Buck's surprise, this growl only tightened the rope further, cutting off his breath. In a rage, Buck leaped at the man. The man threw Buck to the ground, tightening the rope more. Buck fought back furiously. His tongue hung from his mouth. His chest panted for air. Never had he been treated this way. Never had he been so angry. Finally Buck's

strength left him, and his eyes became blank. Later, when the train came, the two men threw him into a baggage car.

The next thing Buck knew, his tongue was hurting, and he was being jolted along in some kind of motion. Then the sound of the train whistle told him that he was on a train. He opened his eyes and stared like a kidnapped king. His royal eyes filled with anger as the man he spotted grabbed for his throat. But Buck was too quick for the man. His jaws bit savagely into the stranger's hand. Then he was choked again, and he blacked out.

Just then a baggage man who had heard their struggle came to check on things. "Yep, the dog has fits," said Buck's captor, as he hid his bloody hand from view. "Takin' him to 'Frisco. Dog doctor there thinks he can cure him." With that, the baggage man left Buck and the stranger alone.

Later that night Buck was taken to a saloon on the San Francisco waterfront. A meeting took place in a shed behind the saloon. There Buck's captor talked with the owner of the saloon about his trip.

"All I get is 50 for it," he grumbled. "I wouldn't do it again for a thousand in cold cash." His hand was wrapped in a bloody rag, and his pants were badly ripped. The kidnapper unwrapped his hand and looked at his injury. "If I don't get rabies from this . . ."

The owner of the saloon only laughed. "If ya don't, it'll be because you were born to hang."

Dazed and in great pain, Buck tried once more to attack his enemies. Again he was thrown down and viciously choked. The men held him down to remove his collar and the rope. Then they threw him into a wooden cage.

Buck lay in the cage for the rest of the night, angry and ashamed. He could not understand what was happening to him. What did these strange men want with him? Why was he being kept in a cage? When he heard the door open again, Buck jumped to his feet. He thought that he was finally going to see his friend the judge again. But it was only the saloon owner looking in at him by the sickly light of a candle. Buck's throat twisted into a growl.

The next morning four men came to pick up Buck's cage. They were evil-looking men, ragged and dirty. These were more men who were bound to hurt him, Buck decided. He snarled at them through the bars of the cage. They only laughed and poked sticks at him. Buck grabbed the sticks with his teeth. But when he saw that the men wanted him to grab the sticks, he quickly lost interest and lay down quietly.

Buck's cage was then lifted into a wagon. From there he began to pass through many hands. Clerks in an office carted him around in another wagon.

Then a truck carried him to a ferryboat. From the boat, he was trucked off to a train station. Finally he was placed in an express car.

For two days and nights, the express car was pulled along by a shrieking engine. The entire time Buck neither ate nor drank. Train clerks would come and go, but Buck greeted them with angry growls. The men reacted by teasing and laughing at him. They barked like dogs, flapped their arms, and howled. It was all very silly, Buck thought. It was an insult to his dignity. But he was glad about one thing—the rope was off his neck. Now he would show them. They would never get a rope around his neck again.

Buck's throat and tongue were sore and raw from lack of water. His bloodshot eyes were filled with anger. By now the judge himself would not have known Buck. The clerks were glad to unload him when the train arrived in Seattle.

Four men carefully carried his cage to a small, walled yard. There a stout man in a loose red sweater signed the driver's book. This was the man, Buck decided. He was the new enemy. Buck flung himself savagely against the bars. The man smiled grimly and picked up a club and a hatchet.

"You ain't going to take him out, are you?" the driver asked.

"Sure," the man answered as he pried at the bars

with the hatchet. Immediately the four other men scattered. Safely on top of the wall, they waited to watch the show.

Meanwhile Buck rushed at the bars, sinking his teeth into the wood. He snarled as the hatchet fell on the cage. Buck wanted to get at the man in the red sweater as much as the man wanted to get at him.

"Now! You red-eyed devil," the man said as he made a large opening in the cage. Then he dropped the hatchet and took the club in his right hand.

Buck was truly a red-eyed devil by now. His hair stood up, his mouth foamed, and his bloodshot eyes glittered. He threw his 140 pounds of fury straight at the man. But in midair, Buck received a blow that jarred his teeth. He whirled over and fell to the ground. He had never been struck with a club in his life. He could not understand what was happening. With a snarl, he rose to his feet and again threw himself at the man. Again a crushing blow sent him to the ground. He was mad with rage. Again and again he charged. Each time the club smashed him down.

After one very hard blow, Buck could only stagger to his feet. He was too weak to attack again. Blood flowed heavily from his nose, mouth, and ears. His beautiful coat was splattered with blood and drool. But the man in the red sweater did not stop. He moved toward Buck again and leveled a frightening smash across his nose. Buck had never known pain like this before. With a lionlike roar, he hurled himself at the man again. But the man just shifted the club to his other hand and caught Buck hard below his jaw. The upward force of the blow sent Buck circling in the air. He crashed to the ground on his head and chest. One last time Buck rushed. Then the man struck a crushing blow that he had been saving for last. Buck went down, knocked cold.

"He's some dogbreaker, I'd say," said one of the men on the wall.

Slowly Buck regained his senses. But he was still too tired and hurt to move. He lay still, watching the man in the red sweater.

"Answers to the name of Buck," the man announced, as he read the note on the wooden crate. "Well, Buck, my boy, we've had our little meeting," he went on. "Best thing now is to let it go at that. You've learned your place, and I know mine. Be a good dog, and all will go well. Be a bad dog, and I'll beat the stuffin' out of you. Understand?"

As he spoke, the man patted Buck's bloodied head. Buck stiffened but was too hurt to move.

When the man brought food and water, Buck ate and drank eagerly. He was beaten—he knew that; but he was not broken. He had learned a lesson that he would not forget for the rest of his life. He saw that he stood no chance against a man with a club. The club, however, was only his first lesson in the rules of survival. Life would be crueler now. But he would face it bravely. He would also face it with all the craftiness he owned.

2 The Law of Club and Fang

As the days passed, other dogs came in crates and at the end of ropes. Some came quietly; others came in a fierce rage, the way Buck had come. Buck watched as each dog fell under the club of the man in the red sweater. Each time Buck learned the lesson all over again. A man with a club is a master to be obeyed.

From time to time, strangers came and talked to the man in the red sweater. After the strangers had paid their money, they left with dogs. Buck wondered where they went, since they never came back. Each time he was glad that it was not he who had been chosen. He was afraid of the unknown.

Finally Buck's time did come, however. One day a little man who spoke broken English saw him. The man cried out, "That one good bully dog! Eh? How much?"

"Three hundred, and a bargain at that," the man in the red sweater replied. "Since it's the government's money, you got no gripe, eh, Perrault?"

Perrault smiled. The price of dogs had gone sky-high. It was a fair price for such a fine animal. Canada would not lose in the deal. With such a dog, government messages would not be slowed down.

Buck watched the money pass between the two men. He was not surprised when he and Curly, a good-natured dog, were led away. The two were loaded on a ship that soon headed north. From the deck, Buck and Curly watched Seattle disappear behind them. It was the last of the warm south either of them would ever see. Perrault turned the dogs over to a giant of a man named François. These men were a new breed to Buck. He did not really like them, but he did respect them. He quickly learned that they were fair men who punished justly. They knew too much about dogs to be fooled by one of them.

Below deck, Buck and Curly met two other dogs. One was a big snow-white fellow. He seemed friendly, but was really sly and tricky. At the first meal, he stole Buck's food. Buck started after the thief. Before he reached him, François's whip flashed through the air. It reached the thief before Buck did. Buck had only to pick up his stolen bone. Watching the way François handled things, Buck's respect for him grew.

Dave, the second dog, wanted only to be left alone. He was a gloomy-looking fellow and let Curly know that there would be trouble if anyone bothered him. He ate and slept, and yawned in between, taking no interest in anything. Buck and

Curly went wild with fear when the boat rolled through rough water. But Dave just raised his head, yawned, and went back to sleep.

Day and night the ship was pushed along by its propellers. One day was much like another. Buck felt the weather grow slowly colder. At last one morning, the engines became quiet. Buck and all the other dogs were excited. Some change was coming.

François put the dogs on leashes and led them onto the shore. Buck's feet sank into something white, soft, and damp. He jumped back. More of this strange white substance was falling through the air.

Buck sniffed at it and licked it with his tongue. At first it stung a bit. In the next second, it was gone. Buck was puzzled. The men laughed at him loudly. He felt ashamed, but he did not know why. Buck had experienced snow for the first time.

Buck's first day on Dyea Beach was a nightmare. Every hour was filled with shock and surprise. Buck, who had suddenly been jerked from a life of care and respect, was thrown into a world of cruelty and violence. Here, there was neither peace nor safety. Life and limb were always in danger. These dogs and men were not town dogs and men. They were savages who knew no law but the law of club and fang.

Buck had never seen dogs fight as these dogs did. Soon he learned a lesson that he would never forget. Curly, in her usual friendly manner, approached a husky the size of a wolf. There was no warning, only a sudden leap and gnash of teeth. In an instant, Curly's face was ripped open from eye to jaw.

Thirty to forty huskies surrounded the two fighters. They stood with a silent passion, licking their chops. Buck did not understand. Curly rushed the husky, who struck again and then leaped aside. On her next rush, Curly was knocked to the ground. She never got up. This was what the other huskies had been waiting for. They all closed in on her, yelping and snarling. Curly was buried, screaming in agony, beneath the mass of attacking dogs.

Buck was stunned by what he had seen. Spitz, a particularly cruel dog, hung out his tongue as if to laugh. Then François, swinging an ax, sprang into the pack. Three other men used their clubs to help scatter the dogs. It did not take long. When the last husky had been clubbed away, Curly lay limp and lifeless in the bloody snow. She had nearly been torn to pieces. François stood over Curly's body and cursed loudly. Often this picture was to come back to disturb Buck's sleep. So that was the way it was. No fair play. Once down, that was the end of you. Well, he would make sure that he never went down. Spitz hung out his tongue and laughed again. From that moment on, Buck bitterly hated Spitz.

Before he could recover from Curly's tragic death, Buck got another shock. François put straps and buckles around him. He had seen horses in such harnesses at home. Now, like the horses, he and the other dogs were strapped together and put to work hauling wood. Buck found this work embarrassing, but he was too wise to rebel. He buckled down and did his best, but it was so strange to him. François demanded that his commands be obeyed immediately. Since he had a whip, all the dogs obeyed.

Dave, who was placed behind Buck, had done this many times before. He nipped at Buck's legs whenever Buck made a mistake. Spitz was the lead dog and was as experienced as Dave. He could not always get at Buck, so he growled and jerked Buck in the direction he should go. Buck learned quickly. He soon knew to stop at *ho* and to go ahead at *mush*.

Perrault was in a hurry to be on the trail to deliver his dispatches. That afternoon he brought in two more dogs, Billie and Joe. They were true huskies. Even though they were brothers, they were as different as day and night. Billie was very good-natured, but Joe was sour and always snarling. Buck welcomed them, but Dave, as usual, paid no attention.

Spitz immediately attacked Billie. When Billie turned to run, Spitz's sharp teeth sank into his side. Knowing he was next, Joe whirled to face Spitz. Joe's hair stood up, his ears lay back, his lips snarled, and his eyes gleamed in a threatening way. Spitz backed away. But to cover his retreat, he turned again on Billie, driving him away.

That evening Perrault brought in another dog. It was an old, tough-looking husky. His battle-scarred face had just one eye. But that eye flashed a warning that other dogs respected. He was called Sol-leks, which means "the angry one." When he marched among the dogs, even Spitz left him alone. Sol-leks did not like dogs to approach him from his blind side. Buck learned this lesson the hard way. When he came up on Sol-leks's blind side, Sol-leks whirled upon him and slashed his shoulder to the bone. From that time forward, Buck kept away from Sol-leks's blind side, and they had no more trouble. Like Dave, Sol-leks seemed to want just one thing—to be left alone. But time would show that both Dave and Sol-leks both wanted something else even more.

3 On the Trail

That night Buck faced the problem of sleeping. When he saw the warm tents aglow with candles, he naturally went inside. But François and Perrault swore and threw things at him. Buck fled into the cold night. The wind nipped sharply at his wounded shoulder. He lay down in the snow, but the cold soon brought him to his feet again. For a time, Buck wandered about in search of a warm place.

Finally an idea came to him. He would see how his teammates were surviving the cold. He looked for them around the camp. To his surprise, they were nowhere to be found. Were they in the tents? No, that could not be possible, since he had been driven out. Then suddenly the snow gave way under him. Something moved under his feet. Buck jumped back and began to snarl. A friendly yelp put him at ease, so he returned to check. A whiff of warm air rose from the ground, and there, curled into a snug ball, was Billie.

Another lesson. So that was the way they did it, eh? Buck chose a spot and began to dig a hole for himself. Shortly his warm body filled the hole, and he was asleep. Buck slept soundly, even though he growled and barked at his bad dreams.

During the night a snowfall buried him completely. In the morning the snow pressed in on him from all sides. For a moment Buck did not know where he was. A great fear swept through him—the wild thing's fear of the trap. It was a fear that came from his untamed ancestors, for he had known nothing of traps in his own life. Buck leapt to his feet with a snarl, sending snow flying all around him. When the snow cleared, he again saw the white camp. Now he remembered where he was and how he got there.

"Wot I say?" shouted François to Perrault. "That Buck for sure learn quick as anything."

Perrault nodded. As a courier carrying important messages for the Canadian government, he was glad to have a dog like Buck.

Three more huskies were added to the team, making a total of nine. All were quickly harnessed and readied for the trip to Dyea Canyon and Dawson. Buck was glad to be going. The work was hard, but he did not hate it. He was surprised to see that all the animals had caught the spirit of excitement. More surprising still was the change in Dave and Sol-leks. In the harness they had become new dogs. Now they were active and alert, eager to begin the journey.

Dave was the dog harnessed closest to the sled.

Buck was in front of Dave. Then came Sol-leks. The rest pulled in a single file behind Spitz, the leader.

Buck had been placed between Dave and Sol-leks so that he might learn from them. They were good teachers, who taught their lessons with their teeth. Dave was a fair and wise one. He nipped at Buck when he made mistakes, but he never nipped without a reason. Once when Buck got tangled in the straps and delayed things, both Dave and Sol-leks gave him a beating. Buck learned quickly. As he learned, the nips became less frequent.

It was a hard day's run across glaciers and snowdrifts, but they made good time. Late that night they pulled into camp at Lake Bennett. Thousands of gold seekers were building boats there. Buck made his hole in the snow and slept the sleep of the weary. But in the early morning darkness, he would again be harnessed with his mates to the sled.

Because the snow was packed on the trail, they had traveled 40 miles the first day. But each day would be harder than the one before as they made their own trail. Perrault had to walk ahead of the team to pack the trail with his snowshoes. For days and days, Buck worked in his harness. Each day started and ended in darkness. The farther they went, the hungrier Buck became. The pound and a half of dried fish he got at the end of the day was never enough, and he was always hungry. The other dogs seemed to do well on even less food. But they weighed less and had been born to that kind of life.

Buck soon lost his old ways of eating. The other dogs ate quickly and then went after Buck's unfinished food. Buck learned to eat as fast as they did. His hunger even drove him to take food from others. He watched and learned. When he saw Pike, a new dog, steal a slice of bacon behind Perrault's back, Buck copied him and got an entire chunk. Dub, a clumsy dog who was always getting caught, was punished for Buck's theft.

The theft showed that Buck was fit to survive in the unfriendly northland. It showed his ability to change. If he had not been able to adapt to his new environment, he would have died. Buck had to put aside his moral nature. Such a thing was fine in the southland, where one lived under the law of love and respect. But in the northland, the law was the law of club and fang. In all his days, he had never run from a fight. The man in the red sweater, however, had taught him a new code. Now he knew to flee to save his hide. He did not steal for the joy of it but because he was starving. He did what he had to do.

Buck's change came about quickly. His muscles became hard as iron. He ignored pain. He could eat anything, no matter how disgusting. Sight and scent became remarkably keen. His hearing was so sharp that even in his sleep he heard the smallest sound. He learned to bite the ice from his toes. And when he was thirsty, he knew how to break the ice to get water to drink. Instincts long dead came to life again. He remembered the time when wild dogs had killed for their meat. It was not hard to learn again how to cut and slash. The tricks of his ancestors came back to him. These thoughts had always been within him. On still, cold nights, Buck howled like a wolf at the stars. It was the long, lonely howl of his distant ancestors.

The beast from the past grew inside Buck, but it grew secretly. He did not pick fights, and he avoided them whenever he could. He never showed his bitter hatred of Spitz through snarls or threatening looks. Spitz, however, never lost a chance to bully Buck or to try to start a fight—a fight that could only have ended in death.

Early in the trip, such a fight almost happened. At the end of the day they had made camp near a frozen lake. The snow and wind cut like a hot knife. To lighten the load, the men had left their tent behind. Here they made their fire and spread their blankets on the ice. Buck made his nest in the snow under an overhanging rock. It was snug and warm inside. Buck hated to leave it when François handed out the thawed fish. When Buck returned, he found that his place had been taken. A snarl quickly told him that the thief was Spitz. Until now Buck had avoided any trouble with Spitz, but this was too much. The beast within him roared. Buck sprang on Spitz with a fury that surprised them both. Spitz had thought that Buck was timid and cowardly.

François was surprised, too. When he saw the cause of the fight, he called to Buck. "Give it to him, by God! Give it to him, the dirty thief!"

Spitz circled back and forth, eager for a chance to spring on Buck. Buck was no less eager and moved around Spitz looking for an opening. It was then that the unexpected happened. Their fight to the death would have to be delayed.

The camp was suddenly alive with prowling, starving huskies. About a hundred of them had crept in while Buck and Spitz were fighting. François and Perrault sprang among the intruders and began to swing their clubs. The wild dogs showed their teeth and fought back. They were crazed by the smell of food. Perrault found one animal with his head in the food box. His club fell hard on its skinny body. The box fell, scattering the bread and bacon. Immediately the starving animals went after the food. They yelped and howled under a rain of blows. But they struggled on madly until each crumb had been eaten.

In the meantime, the surprised team dogs had leapt from their nests. They were immediately attacked by the intruders. Never had Buck seen such dogs. They seemed to be nothing but bones and hide. But their hunger made them terrifying. Buck was attacked by three huskies. In an instant his head and shoulders were badly slashed. Billie was crying as usual. Dave and Sol-leks were dripping blood from many wounds. Joe was snapping like a demon. Buck was sprayed with blood when his teeth cut through the flesh of another dog. The taste of blood only made him fiercer. Then he felt teeth at his own throat. Spitz was attacking him from the side.

Buck shook himself free. Billie sprang through the circle of attackers and ran away across the ice. Pike and Dub followed on his heels. The rest of the team dogs soon followed. As Buck started after them, he spotted Spitz rushing at him. Spitz's bid to knock Buck to the ice failed, and Buck soon joined the fleeing dogs. The nine team dogs, a sorry bunch, gathered in the forest. There was not one who was not badly hurt. Dub had an injured leg. Joe had lost an eye. Dolly, the last dog added to the team, had a torn throat. And the good-natured Billie had a nearly chewed-off ear and cried throughout the night.

In the morning, the dogs limped back to camp. The attackers were gone, but so was half of their food. Nothing worth eating had escaped the starving dogs. They had even eaten Perrault's moose-hide moccasins.

François looked over his wounded dogs. "What you think, eh, Perrault?" he said softly.

Perrault only shook his head. It took two hours to get the wounded team under way. They struggled painfully over the trail. The four hundred hardest miles to Dawson lay ahead of them.

4   A Fight to the Death

It took six days to cross Thirty Mile River. They were terrible days. Every foot of the way was dangerous. Only a few quiet places in this wild river would hold ice. A cold snap had dropped the temperature to 50 below zero. Perrault often broke through the ice. Each time, he had to build a fire to dry his clothes, or he would have died from the cold. Nothing stopped Perrault. He had been chosen as a government courier because of his willingness to take risks.

Once Dave and Buck broke through the ice. They were pulled out half-frozen and nearly drowned. Another time Spitz went through the ice, taking most of the team with him. Only Buck and Dave were left on the edge of the hole. Buck, Dave, and François behind the sled all strained backward. One by one the dogs were pulled from the icy water. They covered only a quarter of a mile that day.

Buck and the rest of the dogs were played out. But Perrault pushed them to make up for lost time. They covered 35 miles the next day, 40 the day after, and 40 the day after that.

Buck's feet were not small and hard like those of

the huskies. The feet of dogs of his breed had become soft since the days of their ancestors. Buck limped along in great pain. In camp he lay down like a dead dog. As hungry as he was, he would not move even to get his fish. François had to bring it to him. After supper François rubbed Buck's feet. He even cut off the tops of his moccasins to make little moccasins for Buck's sore feet. This was a great help. Later, after Buck's feet grew hard, the worn-out footgear was thrown away.

One morning, as they were about to leave, Dolly suddenly went mad. She let out a long howl and then sprang at Buck. He had never seen a dog go mad, so he had no fear of madness. But he knew here was horror, and he fled in panic. Dolly, panting and drooling, was just a leap behind him. They raced through woods and icy streams. As he ran, Buck could hear Dolly's snarls behind him. François called out to Buck, and Buck doubled back to camp, hoping that François would save him. There François stood holding an ax. As Buck shot past him, the ax crashed down on mad Dolly's head.

Buck staggered against the sled, sobbing for breath. Again Spitz saw his chance. He sprang on Buck and sank his teeth to the bone. Suddenly François's whip fell on Spitz. Buck stood by and watched as Spitz received a terrible whipping.

"One devil, that Spitz," said Perrault. "Someday

he'll kill that Buck."

"That Buck two devils," answered François. "Some fine day he'll get mad, and then he'll chew that Spitz all up and spit him out. Sure. I know."

From then on, it was war between Spitz and Buck. Spitz knew that his place as lead dog was being threatened. Buck had surprised him. Other southland dogs were soft and weak, but Buck was different. He matched the huskies in strength and savagery. The man in the red sweater had knocked all rashness out of him. Buck was patient and crafty like the wild dogs of an earlier time.

A fight for leadership would come. Buck wanted to be leader. He had been gripped tight by the pride of the trail, a pride that made dogs work to the last. This pride made Spitz fear Buck as a possible rival. This was Buck's pride, too.

Buck openly challenged Spitz's leadership. One morning after a heavy snowfall, Pike remained hidden in his nest under the snow. He did not come when François called him to the sled. Spitz was wild with anger. He snarled through the camp, looking and digging for Pike. Hearing his snarls, Pike shivered in his hiding place.

When Pike was at last found, Spitz flew at him in a rage. But Buck flew between them with equal rage, throwing Spitz off his feet. Seeing his opportunity, Pike sprang on the leader. Buck, who had long ago forgotten any ideas of fair play, also jumped on Spitz. François chuckled and brought his whip down hard on Buck again and again. Spitz continued to punish Pike.

The days passed, and Dawson grew closer. Buck continued to stand between Spitz and the other dogs. But now he did it when François was not around. Buck's actions made the other dogs dare to rebel. Things went from bad to worse on the team. Trouble was everywhere, and Buck was always at the bottom of it. François knew that sooner or later the two dogs had to fight to the death. Many nights he awoke thinking that he heard Buck and Spitz at it again.

The great fight did not happen. One dreary afternoon they pulled into Dawson. The town was filled with countless men and dogs. Buck saw that the dogs were working. The way of things seemed to be that dogs should always work. Here and there Buck met some southland dogs, but most of the dogs were of the wild, wolf-husky breed. Every night they wailed a weird and eerie song. Buck was happy to join in their howling. He was stirred by these long, drawn-out wailings, which called him back to his beginnings.

Seven days after pulling into Dawson, the men left again with their team. This time they headed for Dyea and Skagway. Perrault had more dispatches to deliver. The team boomed up the Yukon Trail, making 50 miles the first day. But still there was a lot of trouble. Buck's revolt had caused problems within the team. With Buck's protection, the other dogs no longer feared Spitz. One night Pike robbed Spitz of his fish, gulping it down under Buck's protection. Even good-natured Billie no longer whined meekly around Spitz. Buck snarled every time he came near Spitz. Without the control of a leader, the dogs squabbled constantly. Only Dave and Sol-leks remained unchanged.

The fight to the death started the night Dub scared up a rabbit. In a second the whole team was in full cry after it. The rabbit sped down the river, running lightly on the surface of the snow. The dogs had to plow through it. Fifty dogs from a police camp nearby joined the chase. Buck led the pack, but he could not gain on the rabbit. He felt the joy of killing. This was life's summit. Buck felt in the deepest part of his nature that life could hold no more than this. This instinct went back to the beginning of time.

Spitz, cold and crafty even while chasing a kill, left the pack. He cut across a narrow neck of land near a long bend in a creek. Buck did not know this. As he rounded the bend, he saw Spitz. He had leaped into the path of the rabbit, catching it in midair. The rabbit shrieked in terror as the ferocious

white teeth broke its back.

Buck drove at Spitz so hard that he missed his throat. The two dogs rolled over and over in the powdery snow. Spitz was up instantly, slashing Buck down the shoulder. Buck knew the time had come. It would be a fight to the death. The dogs circled, snarling, ears back, each watching for his chance. Over the white woods lay a ghostly calm. Nothing moved. The breaths of the dogs rose slowly in the frosty air.

Spitz had fought many times before. He had mastered every kind of dog. His rage never let him forget that his enemy also felt such rage. Buck's attacks were answered with attacks. Fang clashed with fang, and mouths were cut and bleeding. Time and again Buck tried for Spitz's throat. Each time, Spitz slashed him and got away. Then Buck drew back and drove at Spitz's shoulder like a ram. Again Spitz leaped away, slashing at Buck.

Spitz was unharmed. Buck was bleeding and panting hard. All this time, the other dogs had stood in a silent circle. They were waiting to finish off the dog that went down. As Buck grew winded, Spitz took to rushing him. Once Buck went over. The circle of dogs started toward him, but Buck came around quickly. The circle fell back.

Buck fought by instinct, but he could also fight by head. He rushed at Spitz's shoulder, as he had done before. But at the last instant, he dropped low. His teeth closed on Spitz's left leg. There was the sound of breaking bone. The white dog faced Buck on three legs. Buck repeated the trick and broke Spitz's right leg. In spite of the pain, Spitz struggled to stay up. He saw the circle of eyes and tongues moving toward him.

There was no hope for Spitz. Buck felt no mercy for him as he began his final rush. The circle had closed. Now Buck could feel the breath of the huskies on his own back. He could see them waiting to spring. For a moment nothing happened. Then Spitz staggered back and forth, snarling as if to frighten away death. Buck sprang and met Spitz shoulder to shoulder. The dark circle quickly became a dot on the snow as Spitz disappeared beneath the rush of dogs. Buck was the champion. He had made his kill and found it good.

5 Other Fires, Other Worlds

The morning after the fight, Spitz was missing, and Buck was covered with wounds.

"Eh? What I say? I speak the truth when I say that Buck is two devils," said François.

"That Spitz fight like hell," said Perrault as he looked at Buck's wounds. "Now we make good time. No more Spitz, no more trouble for sure."

While Perrault packed up the camp, François began to harness the dogs. Buck trotted to the lead, where Spitz would normally have been. But François brought Sol-leks forward. Buck sprang on Sol-leks in a fury, driving him back. François slapped his legs and laughed. "Look at that Buck!" he said. "He kills that Spitz, he thinks he take the job. Go 'way!"

Buck would not move. He growled angrily as François dragged him to one side. Again François put Sol-leks in the lead. But as soon as the man turned his back, Buck again drove Sol-leks off.

By now François was angry. "Now, by God, I fix you!" he cried. François picked up a heavy club and moved toward Buck. Buck remembered the man in the red sweater. He moved away from François slowly, snarling with rage. His eyes were fixed on the club. Sol-leks was again put in the lead. François called Buck to his old place in front of Dave, but Buck only moved away. For the better part of an hour, Perrault and François chased after Buck. They threw clubs at him and cursed him. But Buck would not join the team. He was in open revolt. He would be the leader. He had earned the honor, and he would not be satisfied with anything less.

François sat down and scratched his head. Perrault looked at his watch and swore. They were wasting time. They should have been on the trail an hour ago. François could not help grinning. He and Perrault knew that they were beaten. François went to where Sol-leks stood and called Buck. Buck seemed to laugh a kind of dog laugh, but he kept his distance. Even after François put Sol-leks in his old place on the team, Buck still held back.

"Throw down the club," Perrault yelled.

When François had thrown down the club, Buck trotted to the head of the team. Soon the sled dashed onto the trail. Buck quickly took up the duties of leader. François soon learned that Buck was even better than Spitz had been. Buck set about whipping the team into shape. Pike was thrashed for not carrying his load. The first night in camp, Buck punished Joe, something Spitz was never able to do. At Rink Rapids, two new huskies were added to the team. Buck swiftly broke them in.

They were now making record time. The trail was in excellent condition, hard and well packed. The temperature stayed at 50 below zero during the whole trip. Thirty Mile River was covered in just one day. On the 14th day, the lights of Skagway were seen. It had been a record run. For three days Perrault and François were the talk of the town. But before very long, interest turned to other things, and François received new orders. He hugged Buck and wept. And that was the last Buck saw of François and Perrault. They passed out of his life forever.

A Scotsman took charge of the team. With a dozen other teams, they started back to Dawson. The load was heavy, and the work was hard. This was a mail train, carrying news of the world to the men seeking gold.

Buck did not like this job, but he took pride in his work. One day was very much like another. In the morning, fires were built, breakfast was eaten, and dogs were harnessed. Then camp was broken, and they were under way. At night, camp was made, firewood was cut, and dogs were fed. Buck proved his mastery again in three fierce fights with other dogs.

At night Buck loved to lie near the fire. Sometimes he thought of Judge Miller's big house in the sun-kissed southland. But more often he remembered the man in the red sweater. He also remembered the death of Curly and the fight with Spitz. He was not homesick. The sunland was very dim and distant. The memory of his ancestors was far more powerful.

Sometimes as he lay by the fire, Buck seemed to see the flames of another fire. The man by that fire was not the cook but a different man, one with shorter legs, longer arms, and knotty muscles. The man's hair was long and matted. His forehead slanted back. His hand hung midway between knee and foot. In his hand he clutched a stick with a heavy stone on the end. He was naked except for a ragged and fire-scorched animal skin on his back. His body was hairy. He did not walk upright but leaned forward on bent knees.

Beyond the fire Buck seemed to see gleaming coals, two by two, always two by two. Buck knew that these were the eyes of great beasts. He could hear them crashing through the undergrowth. He could hear them making noises in the night. These sights and sounds of another world sometimes made him growl softly. But when the cook shouted, "Hey, Buck, wake up!," the real world came back.

It was a hard trip with heavy work. The dogs were in poor shape when they reached Dawson. They should have had a long rest. But in two days' time, they were loaded up again with letters for the return trip to Skagway. The dogs were tired, and the drivers grumbled. To make things worse, it snowed every day. The soft snow made the pulling even harder. The strength of the dogs disappeared. Since the beginning of the winter, they had dragged sleds 1,800 miles. Billie cried and whimpered in his sleep each night. Joe was more upset than ever. No one dared to get near Sol-leks, blind side or other side. Buck, too, was very tired.

It was Dave who suffered most of all. Something had gone wrong with him. He became depressed and cranky. When camp was made, he quickly made his nest and did not get on his feet again until morning. If the sled stopped suddenly or jerked, he would cry out in pain. One night the drivers brought Dave out to the fire. They could see nothing wrong, but when they pressed or poked, he cried out. Something was wrong inside.

Before long Dave was falling in his harnesses often. The Scotsman took him out of the team to let him get some rest. Dave growled as Sol-leks was put in his place nearest the sled. When the sled started to move, Dave jumped at Sol-leks, trying to throw him off into the snow. He yelped and cried with pain as he tried to take back his old place. His strength was gone, and he staggered along behind the sled to the next stop. When the driver tried to start the sled again, the dogs swung out easily. But the sled did

not move. Dave had bitten through Sol-leks's
harness and was standing in front of the sled.
He begged with his eyes to go back to his old
place.

The driver was puzzled. The men talked of dogs
they had known that died from lack of work,
although that work would have killed them. They
decided that since Dave was to die anyway,
he should die in the harness. He was put back in
his place on the team. Several times he fell down,
and once the sled ran over his legs. Thereafter he
limped on one of his hind legs.

More than once Dave cried out in pain. But he

held out until camp was reached. In the morning he was too weak to travel. He tried to crawl to his driver, then staggered slowly to where the dogs were being harnessed. The last his teammates saw of him, he lay gasping in the snow. But they could hear his mournful howl until they reached a belt of trees.

The team stopped, and the Scotsman walked back to the camp. The other men stopped talking. A pistol shot rang out. When the Scotsman returned, whips snapped, and the sleds began plowing along the trail. Buck knew, and every dog knew, what had happened behind the belt of trees.

6   Sold for a Song

Thirty days after leaving Dawson, the mail arrived at Skagway. The dogs were in a wretched state, worn out and worn down. Pike and Sol-leks limped badly, and Dub suffered from an injured shoulder. All of them were footsore and thin. Their strength had been used up, every last bit of it. There was no spring in their feet as they tottered down the main street of the town. They were dead tired.

The drivers had looked forward to a long stopover. But so many men had rushed north looking for gold, and so many relatives had been left behind. The mail was piled high, and orders were waiting. Fresh dogs were to take the places of the worthless ones. In a few days, Buck and his teammates were sold, harnesses and all. The Scotsman and the other men passed out of Buck's life just as Perrault and François had.

The new owners were from the States and called each other Hal and Charles. Charles was a weak-looking man with weak eyes and a turned-up moustache. Hal was just 19 or 20 and carried a big revolver and a hunting knife on his belt. Both men looked very much out of place.

When Buck and his teammates were driven to the new owners' camp, Buck saw a sloppy mess. The tent was not stretched, the dishes were not washed, and everything was in disorder. Buck also saw a woman the men called Mercedes. She was Charles's wife and Hal's sister.

Buck watched as they started to load the sled. They rolled the tent into a bundle three times as large as it should have been. They packed unwashed tin dishes. Throughout all this, Mercedes fluttered about giving advice. When a clothes sack was loaded on the front, she wanted it on the back. When the men covered it over, she found more things she wanted to pack in that very sack.

Three men from a nearby tent looked on grinning and winking at one another. "I wouldn't tote that tent along if I was you," said one.

"What!" Mercedes cried. "However in the world could I manage without a tent?"

"It's springtime, so you won't get any more cold weather," the man replied.

"Think it'll ride?" another man asked. "Seems a bit top-heavy."

At that, Hal swung his whip and shouted, "Mush! Mush on there!"

The dogs strained hard but could not move the sled. As Hal raised his whip to lash them again, Mercedes cried, "Oh, Hal, you mustn't." Then she grabbed the whip from his hand. "The poor dears! You must promise not to be mean to them, or I won't go a step."

"Precious little you know about dogs," her brother said. "They're lazy. You've got to whip them."

"They're weak as water if you want to know," one of the men said. "They need a rest."

"Rest be blanked," Hal said. He took the whip and cracked it again and again over the dogs. They were still unable to pull the sled.

One of the men could keep quiet no longer. "It's not that I care a whoop what becomes of you, but I care about the dogs. Your runners are froze fast. Throw your weight against it right and left and break it out."

Hal followed his advice, and the overloaded sled moved ahead. But as they were going down a steep slope toward the main street, the sled tipped over. The dogs broke into a run, pulling the sled on its side. The contents scattered wildly along the main street of Skagway.

Kind-hearted citizens caught the dogs and picked up the belongings. They also gave the new drivers some advice. Half the load and twice the dogs if they expected to reach Dawson was what they said. Men laughed as canned goods and thick blankets were unloaded.

"Throw away that tent and all those dishes. Who's

going to wash them?" one of the men said.

Charles and Hal went out that evening and bought six more dogs. This brought the team to 14. These new dogs did not seem to know anything. Buck could teach them what not to do but not what to do. They did not take kindly to the harness and the trail. With these newcomers and the worn-out old team, things did not look bright.

The two men, however, were quite proud and cheerful. Their team was larger than any they had seen. But there was a reason why they had never seen 14 dogs in a team. One sled could not carry enough food for 14 dogs. But Charles and Hal did not know this.

The next morning Buck led the long team up the street. There was no snap to their steps. They were dead weary, and they had no faith in their masters. As the days went by, it became clear that their masters did not know how to do anything. It took them half the night to pitch camp. The sled was packed so poorly that they had to stop often to fix the load. On some days they did not make ten miles. On other days they were unable even to get started. And at no time did they cover the distance they had used in figuring the amount of dog food they needed. To make matters worse, they overfed the dogs. Mercedes, with tears in her eyes, begged Hal to feed them even more. But it was not food that

Buck and the huskies needed. It was rest.

Hal awoke one day and realized that the dog food was half gone. They had gone only a quarter of the way to Dawson. Hal cut back on the food and tried to increase the day's travel.

The first to go was Dub. His shoulder had gone from bad to worse. Finally Hal shot him with his big revolver. Next the new dogs, not used to having so little food, began to die. Mercedes no longer wept over the dogs. She wept for herself. The two men and the woman argued all the time. They lacked the patience of those who worked and suffered in the Arctic. They argued over who did more work or who should chop a few sticks for the fire. So the fire remained unbuilt, the camp half-pitched, and the dogs unfed.

Mercedes was particularly quarrelsome. It was her habit to be helpless. She was sore and tired and insisted on riding on the sled. This extra 120 pounds added the last straw to the load. She rode for days until the weak and starving dogs fell in their harnesses. The sled stood still. Charles and Hal begged her to get off and walk. Mercedes just cried and called them brutes.

Once the men picked Mercedes up and took her from the sled by force. They never did it again. She let her legs go limp like a spoiled child and sat on the trail. After traveling on for three miles, they went back for her and put her on the sled again.

In their misery, the men ignored the animals. The food was now gone. Buck staggered along at the head of the team as if in a nightmare. He fell often and stayed down until a whip brought him up again. His limp hair was matted with blood. Each rib and every bone was outlined on his skin. But Buck's heart was unbreakable. The man in the red sweater had proved that.

Like Buck, the other six dogs were walking skeletons. There came a day when Billie fell and could not get up. Hal took the ax and knocked Billie on the head. Buck and the other dogs knew that the same fate awaited them. The next day another teammate died. Only five dogs remained. All were crippled and limping. The spring weather was beautiful, but neither dogs nor humans were aware of it. Dawn came at three in the morning, and twilight lasted until nine at night. Wedges of wild fowl flew overhead. From every hill came the trickle of running water. Everything was thawing. Cracks formed in the ice, and thin pieces of ice fell into the river. Throughout this Arctic spring, humans and dogs staggered into John Thornton's camp at White River. Buck's group arrived late in the season.

Hal did all the talking. John Thornton sat quietly whittling an ax handle. He gave short answers to their questions and offered little advice because he knew it would not be followed. Thornton warned them to take no more chances on the melting ice.

Hal sneered, "They told us we couldn't make White River, but here we are."

"Only fools with a fool's luck could have made it," Thornton replied. "I tell you straight, I wouldn't risk that ice for all the gold in Alaska."

"That's because you're not a fool, I suppose," Hal said. "All the same, we're going to Dawson." Then, uncoiling his whip, he yelled, "Get up there, Buck! Get up! Mush on!"

The team did not move. The whip flashed again and again. Sol-leks was the first to crawl to his feet. The others followed slowly. But not Buck. He lay quietly where he had fallen. The whip fell on him again and again.

Hal flew into a rage and picked up the club. Blow after blow rained down on Buck. Still he would not move. He had suffered so much that the blows no longer hurt much. The spark of life flickered in him and went down. He was numb to the pain. He could hear the club hit him, but he felt nothing.

Without warning, John Thornton let out a cry. He sprang on Hal and hurled him backward. Mercedes screamed, but Charles was too stiff to move.

"If you strike that dog again, I'll kill you," he said in a choking voice.

Hal drew his long hunting knife. Thornton rapped

Hal's hand with the ax handle, and the knife fell to
the ground. He rapped him again when he tried to
pick it up. Then Thornton picked up the knife and
with two quick strokes cut Buck's harness.

Hal had no fight left in him. A few minutes later,
the two men, one woman, and the four dogs started
across the thawing river.

As Buck watched them leave, Thornton knelt
beside him. His rough but kind hands felt for broken
bones. Nothing was broken, just bruises and
starvation. Dog and man watched the sled crawl
over the ice. Suddenly they saw its back end drop

down. Mercedes's scream came to their ears. A large piece of ice gave way, then dogs and humans disappeared.

Thornton and Buck looked at each other.

"You poor devil," John said, and Buck licked his hand affectionately.

7 A New Life

John Thornton's feet had frozen the previous December on the way to Dawson. His partners had made him comfortable and had gone on. They promised to return with a raft to carry him to Dawson. Lying on the riverbank through the long spring days, John's pain left him. Buck, too, slowly won back his strength. The four of them—Buck, John Thornton, Skeet, and Nig—loafed lazily as they waited for the raft. Skeet was a little Irish setter who quickly made friends with Buck. She had a doctor quality about her. As Buck lay near death, she washed his wounds the way a mother cat washed her kittens. Nig was equally friendly but somewhat shy. He was half bloodhound and half deerhound, with laughing eyes that showed his good nature.

To Buck's surprise, these dogs showed no jealousy toward him. They seemed to share the kindness of John Thornton. As Buck grew stronger, he romped and played with Skeet and Nig. Even Thornton joined in all sorts of silly games. This was a new life for Buck. Love, genuine love, was his for the first time. This he had never known, even with Judge Miller. With the judge, there had been a noble

friendship. But John Thornton had aroused in Buck a love and devotion that was new to him.

This man had saved his life. But more than that, he was the ideal master. Others looked after their dogs out of a sense of duty or business. John cared for his dogs as though they were his children. He had a way of taking Buck's head roughly between his hands and drawing it close to his own. Buck knew no greater joy.

Buck's love was expressed in adoration. Unlike Skeet and Nig, Buck never shoved his nose under Thornton's hand or rested his head on his knee. Buck was content to keep his distance. He would lie for hours at Thornton's feet. Or sometimes he would lie farther away, watching Thornton's movements. So strong was their union that Buck's gaze would cause Thornton to turn his head. The two would look at each other without speaking. But their hearts shined through their eyes.

For a long time, Buck would not allow Thornton out of his sight. Other masters had come and gone. He feared that Thornton would also pass out of his life. Even at night, Buck was troubled by this fear. He would often creep to his master's tent and stand by the flap.

In spite of this love for Thornton, Buck's primitive fury was still strong. Buck had become a creature of the wild northland. Nothing of the soft southland remained in him. But he would not steal from this man or attack his dogs. To any other man or any other dog, he showed no mercy. He had learned well the law of club and fang. Kill or be killed, eat or be eaten was the law.

The past and the present were linked in Buck. The past pounded in him with a mighty rhythm. He sat, white fanged and long furred, by John Thornton's fire. But behind him were the shades of half wolves and wild wolves. Each day the claims of mankind slipped further away. Deep in the forest, a call was sounding. Whenever Buck heard it, he felt driven to leave the fire and plunge into the forest. But his love for John Thornton always drew him back to the fire.

When Thornton's partners, Hans and Pete, arrived on their raft, Buck refused to have anything to do with them. After learning that they were friends, he put up with them, but he never showed them any affection. By the time they reached Dawson, Hans and Pete understood Buck and his ways. For Thornton, however, Buck's love seemed to grow and grow. Thornton alone could put a pack on Buck's back. Nothing was too great for Buck to do if Thornton commanded it. One day the men and the dogs were sitting on a tall cliff that dropped some three hundred feet straight down. Thornton sat on the edge with and Buck at his side.

On a whim, Thornton got the attention of Hans and Pete. Then he commanded, "Jump, Buck!" The next instant he was wrestling with Buck on the edge of the cliff. Hans and Pete dragged them back to safety.

"It's eerie," Pete said.

Thornton shook his head. "No, its wonderful," he said. "It sometimes makes me afraid."

"I wouldn't want to be the man that bothers you when he's around," Pete added.

Before the year was out, Pete's worries were realized. "Black" Burton, a bad-tempered man, had been picking a fight with a newcomer in the bar. Thornton stepped between the men good-naturedly.

Buck, as usual, was lying in a corner watching his master. Without warning, Burton threw a fist straight from his shoulder. Thornton was sent spinning into the bar.

Buck roared when he saw this and flew through the air for Burton's throat. The man threw out his arm but was hurled backward to the floor. Buck let go of the arm and again went for the throat. This time Buck caught it and tore it open. Quickly the crowd drove Buck off. While the doctor checked the bleeding, Buck growled furiously. He was kept away by the men's hostile clubs. A meeting was held on the spot. It was decided that Buck had a right to attack. From that day on, Buck's fame spread through every camp in Alaska.

Later, in the fall, Buck saved Thornton's life in another way. The three men were going down a bad stretch of rapids on Forty Mile Creek. Thornton was in the boat, guiding it with a pole. Hans and Pete moved along the bank holding the boat with ropes tied to trees. On the bank, Buck watched his master anxiously. At a particularly bad spot, Hans tried to slow the boat with the rope. But he jerked the rope too soon, and the boat flipped bottom up. Thornton was thrown into the churning water. It swiftly carried him to the wildest part of the rapids. No swimmer could survive in that current.

Buck instantly sprang into the rapids. In a mad

swirl of water, he reached Thornton. When he felt Thornton grab his tail, Buck swam for the bank. Even with all his strength, Buck could move only very slowly toward shore. The man and the dog were moving downstream rapidly. They heard the water below roaring through jagged rocks that looked like the teeth of a huge comb. Thornton knew the shore was impossible to reach. He scraped across several rocks and struck a third violently. He let go of Buck and held fast to the slippery rock. "Go, Buck! Go!" he shouted.

Buck swam to the shore, where Pete and Hans dragged him from the water. They knew that Thornton could not hold the rock for very long. They ran up the bank to a place that was far upstream from Thornton. There they tied a rope carefully around Buck's neck and shoulders. Buck jumped into the stream and swam for Thornton. But the stream carried him faster than he expected. Buck passed helplessly out of Thornton's reach.

Hans pulled Buck back through the water to the bank. When he reached Hans and Pete, Buck was half-drowned. He staggered to his feet then fell down. Thornton's voice could be heard faintly. Hearing it, Buck sprang to his feet and ran again to the edge of the water. Again he struck out for Thornton. This time he would not make a mistake. Hans let out the rope while Pete kept it from twisting. Thornton saw Buck coming at him. Buck struck him with the force of the current behind him. Thornton reached up and put both arms around Buck's shaggy neck. When Hans wrapped the rope around the tree, they were both pulled underwater. Choking and smashing against rocks, they veered toward shore.

Thornton came to, face down, on the bank. Buck's limp and seemingly lifeless body lay nearby. Slowly Buck also came around. Thornton, who was himself bruised and battered, felt Buck's body and found three broken ribs.

"That settles it," he announced. "We camp right here." And camp they did until Buck's ribs healed. When man and dog were mended, the group was able to travel again.

8 For the Love of a Man

That winter, at Dawson, Buck performed another heroic deed. This one was perhaps not as dangerous, but it was one that made his fame grow even more. It was a particularly happy deed for three men. Buck made it possible for them to make a trip to the east, where so far no gold miners had gone.

It started in the Eldorado Saloon, where men bragged about their favorite dogs. Buck, because of his fame, was being ridiculed. Thornton was driven to defend Buck's strength. One man said that his dog could pull a sled with five hundred pounds on it. A second man claimed six hundred pounds for his dog; and a third man, seven hundred.

"Pooh!" John Thornton said. "Buck can move a thousand pounds."

"And walk off with it for a hundred yards?" a man named Matthewson demanded. He was the one who had claimed seven hundred pounds for his dog.

"And walk off with it for a hundred yards," Thornton said coolly.

"Well," Matthewson said slowly. "I've got a thousand dollars that says he can't. And there it is."

As he spoke, he slammed a sack of gold dust on the bar.

Nobody spoke. Thornton's bluff, if it was a bluff, had been called. He felt his blood rush to his face. His tongue had tricked him. He did not know whether Buck could move a thousand pounds. Half a ton! The eyes of a dozen men stared at him silently. What was more, he did not have a thousand dollars. Neither did Hans or Pete.

"I've got a sled outside now," Matthewson went on. "It has 20 fifty-pound sacks of flour on it."

Thornton did not answer. He did not know what to say. He glanced from face to face looking for an answer. Jim O'Brien, an old friend, caught his eye. Seeing him, Thornton did what he would never have dreamed of doing.

"Can you lend me a thousand?" he asked softly.

"Sure," O'Brien answered. He thumped down a sack of gold dust. "Though there's little chance, I'm given that the dog can do it."

The men streamed out of the Eldorado to see the test. Several hundred men in furs and mittens crowded around the sled. Matthewson's sled with its thousand pounds had been standing there for hours. In the 60-below-zero cold, the runners had frozen fast to the snow. Even at three-to-one odds, not one man bet on Buck. Thornton had been rushed into the bet. Now as he looked at the sled, the task seemed impossible. Matthewson was overjoyed.

"Three to one!" he shouted. "I'll bet you another thousand, Thornton. What d'you say?"

Thornton's fighting spirit was aroused. He forgot how impossible the task looked. This was a battle. He called Hans and Pete to his side. Together the three men had only two hundred dollars. Without stopping to think, they put it up against Matthewson's six hundred.

Matthewson's team was unhitched, and Buck was put onto the sled. He caught the excitement. He felt in some way that he had to do a great thing for Thornton. The men murmured as they watched this splendid animal. Buck was in perfect condition. He was 150 pounds of grit. His coat shone like silk. His mane bristled. Tight muscles rolled below the skin. After some of the men had felt these ironlike muscles, the odds dropped to two to one.

"Gad, sir!" stuttered one man. "I give you eight hundred dollars for him, just as he stands."

Thornton shook his head and stepped to Buck's side. The crowd became quiet except for the gamblers offering odds. Thornton took Buck's head in his hands and held it next to his. "As you love me, Buck. As you love me," he whispered. Buck whined eagerly.

The crowd watched this strange affair. Buck took

Thornton's mittened hand softly in his mouth. Then he let it go slowly. Thornton stepped back and said, "Now, Buck!"

Buck swung to the right, taking up the slack in the harness. His 150 pounds stopped with a jerk. From under the sled's runners rose a crisp crackling sound.

"Haw!" Thornton commanded. Buck plunged again, this time to the left. The crackling turned to snapping as the runners slipped several inches to the side. The sled was broken out. The men saw it and held their breath.

"Now, mush!" Thornton yelled.

Thornton's command cracked like a pistol shot. Buck threw himself forward. The harness tightened with a jerk. His muscles knotted under his fur. His head leaned forward while his feet clawed at the hard snow. The sled swayed and half started forward. One of his feet slipped, and a man groaned out loud. Then the sled lurched ahead. It moved in a rapid series of jerks—half an inch, one inch, two inches. The jerks decreased until the sled moved steadily along.

Men gasped, then began to breath again. Thornton was running behind the sled. He encouraged Buck with his cheery words. A pile of firewood marked the end of the hundred yards. A cheer grew into a roar as Buck passed the firewood.

Every man, even Matthewson, let out a yell. Hats and mittens were flying in the air. Men were shaking hands all around in a babel of noise. Thornton fell on his knees beside Buck and held the dog's head against his own.

"Gad, sir! Gad, sir!" spluttered the man who had offered $800 for Buck. "I'll give you $1,000 for him, sir; $1,000, sir; $1,200."

Thornton rose to his feet. His eyes were wet. "Sir," he said. "You can go to hell."

Buck took Thornton's hand in his teeth. Thornton shook him back and forth. The onlookers drew back. They knew not to intrude on such a moment.

9 The Call

Thornton used the money Buck had won for him to pay off some debts. More important, the money made it possible for him to journey to the east. There Thornton would search for the famous lost gold mine. For as long as anyone could remember, stories had been told about this mine. Many men had looked for it. Few had found it. More than a few never returned. The lost mine was wrapped in tragedy and mystery. It seemed that an old cabin had always figured in these stories about the mine. Dying men had sworn that this cabin marked the site of the mine. The proof was in the gold nuggets they carried.

No living man had such gold, and the dead were dead. So John Thornton, Pete, Hans, and Buck and six other dogs turned east. They sledded 70 miles up an unknown part of the Yukon Trail. They went up the Steward River until it narrowed into a small stream.

John Thornton asked little of man or nature. He was unafraid of the wild. Being in no hurry, he hunted his dinner along the way. His load was largely ammunition and tools.

The trip was pure joy to Buck. He loved this hunting, fishing, and wandering through strange places. Day after day, week after week, they would set up camp, build a fire, and eat what they could find. Depending on the hunt, they either feasted or starved. Summer came, and dogs and men rafted across lakes and rivers.

The months came and went. Back and forth the men wound through the vast, unknown spaces. In the summer they shivered through the midnight sun. In the fall they entered a lake country, sad and silent. They found no sign of life there, only the blowing winds. Through another winter they wandered over lost trails. Once they came upon an old path in the forest and thought that the lost cabin was near. But the path ended nowhere. Another time they happened upon the wreckage of a lodge, where Thornton found a long-barreled rifle. The men knew that the gun had been left there in the early days, but that was all. No hint of the man who had left it remained.

Spring came again. The men did not find the lost cabin, but they did find gold. It lay with the sand and gravel left by an ancient glacier. They searched no further. The gold looked like butter in the bottom of their pans. Each day's find was worth thousands of dollars. The men packed the gold in moose-hide bags and stacked them outside like firewood.

There was little for the dogs to do now. Buck spent long hours dreaming by the fire. He often had visions of following at the heels of a short, stooped, hairy man. The most notable thing about that rough man's world was fear. The man's sleep was restless. He woke up often, staring into the darkness. He searched for hidden danger as he walked. Buck followed the man noiselessly through the forest. Both were alert to the sounds and smells around them. The man's senses were as keen as Buck's. Their noses quivered; their ears twitched.

Along with this vision of the hairy man was the call sounding in the forest. It filled Buck with strange desires. It made him feel a wild yearning for he knew not what. Sometimes he dashed into the forest, as if looking for something. He pushed his nose into the soil and snorted at the earth smells. He hid behind fallen trees as if to surprise this call. He did not know why he did these things, but he seemed driven to do them. Lying in camp dozing, he would sometimes spring to his feet. Then he dashed for hours through woods and open spaces. For a day at a time, he would lie in the underbrush watching the birds. Most of all he loved running at twilight, seeking the mysterious something that called him.

One night Buck sprang from his sleep with a start. From the forest rose a long, drawn-out howl. Buck's nostrils quivered. His mane bristled in waves. He had heard that sound before. Buck dashed swiftly through the sleeping camp and into the woods. As he drew closer to the cry, he slowed down. Cautiously he moved to a clearing in the woods. Looking out, he saw a long, lean timber wolf. The animal stood erect with his nose pointing to the sky.

The wolf, sensing Buck's presence, stopped howling. Buck stalked into the open, his body crouching, his tail straight and stiff. Every move seemed both friendly and threatening. It was the truce that marks the meeting of wild beasts. But the wolf fled at the sight of Buck. Buck followed in a frenzy to overtake him. He ran the wolf into the bed of a dry creek, where a pile of timber barred the way. Snarling and snapping his teeth, the wolf whirled about like a cornered husky.

Buck circled but did not attack. Buck was three times the size of the wolf. The wolf's head barely reached Buck's shoulder. Seeing his chance, the wolf dashed away, and the chase continued. Time and again he was cornered only to repeat the escape. He would run until Buck drew even with his flanks. Then he would whirl around and flee again.

Finally, feeling no harm was meant, the wolf turned and sniffed noses with Buck. They became friendly and played about uneasily. After a time, the wolf started off as if going somewhere. Buck followed, and they ran side by side through the

creek bed. On the other side were great stretches of forest crossed by streams. Hour after hour they ran. Buck was wildly happy. At last he was answering the call. Running by the side of his wild brother, old memories were returning. Somewhere in that other world, he had done this before. Now he was again running free in the open.

The animals stopped to drink from a running stream. Remembering John Thornton, Buck sat down. The wolf started off again. Then he returned to Buck and sniffed his nose as if to ask him to follow. But Buck turned around and started slowly back to camp. For an hour his wild brother ran with him, whining softly. Then the wolf sat down, pointed his nose upward, and howled. It was a sad howl. As Buck continued on, the howl grew fainter and fainter until it was lost in the distance.

10 Ghost Dog

For two days after his experience with the wolf, Buck did not let Thornton out of his sight. He followed him about his work. He watched him when he ate and slept. But on the third day, he again heard the call from the forest. Now it was stronger than ever. Buck was haunted by thoughts of his wild brother and of the land beyond the creek bed. Once again he took to the woods, but his brother came no more. Buck listened in vain for his long, sad howl.

Buck began to stay away from camp for days. Once he crossed the creek and wandered for a week. But he found no signs of the wild brother. Buck fished for salmon and hunted animals. He killed a large black bear that was blinded by mosquitoes. It was a hard fight that aroused all of Buck's rage.

Buck's thirst for blood became stronger than ever before. Buck had become a killer, an animal that lived on other living creatures. He needed only his own strength and skill to survive. Here, where only the strong survived, he was master. He was possessed of a great pride. It showed in all his movements, in his muscles, even in his coat. Except for the white on his chest, he looked like a giant wolf. His Saint Bernard father had given him size and weight. His shepherd mother, however, had given shape to that size and weight.

Buck had the cunning of a wolf. But his intelligence was that of a Saint Bernard and a shepherd. He had been taught in the fierce schools of the north. Now he was as dreaded as any animal in the wild. Every part of brain and body was keyed to a high pitch. His muscles were as taut as steel springs. He responded to sights and sounds with lightning speed.

"Never was there such a dog," John Thornton said as Buck ran out of camp.

"He's one of a kind," Pete answered.

"By jingo! I think so," Hans agreed.

The men did not see the terrible change that occurred in the darkness of the forest. There Buck became a thing of the wild. He knew how to crawl like a snake; and like a snake, how to strike. He could kill a rabbit as it slept and catch a chipmunk in midair. Neither fish nor beaver was too quick for him. He killed to eat, and he alone ate what he killed.

As fall came on, moose began to appear in great numbers. They moved slowly into the valleys. Buck had already killed a large calf. Now he wished for stronger and larger prey. He came upon it one day when 20 moose moved into the valley. Among them was a great bull. He stood six feet high and had a savage temper. His antlers stretched seven feet from tip to tip. His eyes burned as he roared at the sight of Buck. A feathered arrow in his side explained his savagery.

Buck started to cut the bull away from the herd. He barked and danced just out of reach of the antlers and hoofs. The bull charged, and Buck leapt aside. Slowly the bull was lured from the herd. But then the younger bulls charged Buck, and the wounded bull returned to the herd.

Buck had the patience of the wild. He clung to the herd, driving the wounded bull mad with rage. For half a day, this attacking from all sides went on. In time the younger bulls grew tired of aiding their leader. By twilight the old bull stood alone. He watched his mates leave in the fading light. The fanged terror would not let him follow. He had lived a long, strong life, full of fight. In the end he faced death from a creature that did not even reach his knees.

From then on, night and day, Buck never gave the bull a moment's rest. He never allowed him to eat or drink. Often the bull tried hopelessly to flee. Buck did not try to stop his flights. Instead he loped easily at his heels. But Buck attacked the bull fiercely whenever he tried to eat or drink.

The bull's great head drooped under its tree of horns. His efforts to escape grew weaker, and Buck found more time to get water or to rest himself. On the fourth day, he pulled the moose down. For a day and a night, he stayed with the kill. Then, rested and strong, he turned toward camp and John Thornton. As he moved, Buck felt a new stir in the land. There was new life in it. It was a life different from the life that had been there before. The birds talked of it. The breeze whispered it. There was a message in the very air he breathed. A sense of disaster weighed on him.

Three miles from camp, Buck came upon a fresh trail. It sent the hair on his neck bristling. The trail led straight toward the camp and John Thornton. Tense and alert, Buck hurried on cautiously. The forest was silent. The birds were gone. The squirrels were in hiding. As Buck slid along like a shadow, his nose jerked suddenly. He followed the scent into a thicket, where he found Nig lying on his side, dead. An arrow stuck from either side of his body. Farther on, Buck came upon one of the sled dogs thrashing and near death.

From the camp came the faint chant of many voices. Crawling forward to the edge of the camp, Buck found Hans lying facedown. His body was so feathered with arrows that he looked like a porcupine. Then Buck saw something that made his hair leap straight up. A gust of rage swept over him. He growled with a terrible ferocity. For the last time in his life, he let passion rule his reason. Because of his great love for John Thornton, Buck lost his head.

The Yeehats were dancing about the camp when they heard the fearful roar. An animal unlike any they had ever seen rushed upon them. It was Buck, a hurricane of fury. He sprang at the first man, the chief of the Yeehats, and Buck ripped his throat wide open. A fountain of blood spouted forth. With the next leap, he tore wide the throat of a second man. Buck plunged about in the midst of the enemy, tearing and destroying. So entangled were they that the Indians shot one another with their arrows. A spear aimed at Buck drove through the chest of a hunter. The Yeehats fled in panic to the woods, shouting of the evil spirit.

Buck truly was the evil spirit. He raged at their heels, dragging them down like deer. They scattered far and wide. Buck, weary of the fight, returned to camp. He found Pete dead in his blankets. The earth told of Thornton's hopeless struggle. Skeet lay dead, head and front feet in the stream, faithful to the last. Hidden in the muddy water lay John Thornton. Buck had followed his tracks into the water. No tracks led out.

All day Buck roamed about the camp. He knew death, and he knew that John Thornton was dead. Buck felt an aching emptiness in his heart. When he stared at the bodies of the Yeehats, he forgot the pain. At times he took great pride in himself. He had killed man, the noblest game of all. He sniffed at their bodies. They had died easily. It was harder to kill a husky. Were it not for their arrows and spears, they would be no match. Thereafter he would not fear them except when they carried weapons.

The call of the forest came to Buck louder than ever before. Now he was ready to obey. John Thornton was dead. The last tie was broken. Buck was no longer bound to man.

Hunting moose as the Yeehats had, the wolf pack came to Buck's valley. They poured in a silvery flood into the clearing. Buck stood waiting. The wolves were amazed, so large and still he stood. In a moment the boldest one leaped for Buck. Like a flash Buck struck, breaking the wolf's neck. Three others tried. But one by one they drew back, bleeding from slashed throats. Seeing this, the whole pack sprang forward. Buck whirled on his hind legs, snapping and gashing. He was everywhere at once. Slowly he was forced backward against a high bank. Protected on three sides, he faced them. So well did he face them that the wolves finally retreated with their tongues hanging from their mouths. White fangs shone cruelly in the moonlight. One wolf, long and lean and gray, came forward. Buck recognized the wild brother with whom he had run. They whined softly and touched noses.

Then an old battle-scarred wolf came forward. Buck began to snarl but then sniffed noses with him, too. The old wolf pointed his nose to the moon and broke into a howl. The others sat and howled. And now the call came back to Buck. He, too, began to howl. When they had finished, the pack crowded around Buck and sniffed him. Their manner was half-friendly and half-savage. The leaders raised a yelp and sprang away into the woods. The rest of the pack swung in behind them. Buck ran with them, side by side with his wild brother.

Here may well end the story of Buck. After a few years, the Yeehats noted a change in the timber wolves. Some showed a patch of white fur down their chest. The Yeehats tell of a frightening ghost dog that runs at the head of the pack. His cunning is greater than their own. The fearful animal steals from their camps, robs their traps, and slays their dogs.

The tale grows even worse. There are Yeehat hunters who fail to return. There are some who are found with throats slashed. The footprints left in the snow are greater than those of any wolf.

There is a certain valley that the Yeehats never enter. In the summers, however, a certain visitor comes to the valley. It is a great wolf, like and yet unlike all other wolves. He comes alone to the open space among the trees. Here a yellow stream flows through rotten moose-hide sacks. The wolf stands for a time, howls once, and then leaves. The animal is not always alone. He may also be seen running at the head of the pack through the moonlight.